The Real Price of

The story of Scotland's Fishing Industry and Communities

Linda Fitzpatrick

Westro **INS20 at Lochinver on her maiden trip, 1992.**

Contents

© The Scottish Fisheries Museum, 2010
First Published in the United Kingdom, 2010
Stenlake Publishing Limited
54-58 Mill Square, Catrine, KA5 6RD

Telephone: 01290 551122
www.stenlake.co.uk
enquiries@stenlake.co.uk

ISBN 9781840334876
Reprinted 2013
Printed in China

Fishing from the Earliest Times

TYPES OF FISH

Different varieties of fish can be classified in a number of ways but for the purposes of the fishing industry, the most useful distinction is habitat; where the fish live and how they feed determines where and how they can be caught. Fish (other than crustaceans or shellfish) therefore are generally divided into two groups: pelagic fish such as herring, mackerel and sprats (which swim in surface waters) and demersal fish such as cod, haddock, hake and flatfish, which swim near the seabed.

Haddock.

Most pelagic fish feed on microscopic plants and animals such as plankton which flourish in surface waters. Demersal fish, on the other hand, live on small fish and crustaceans found on the seabed. Pelagic fish are also known as oily fish (those particularly rich in omega oils) and demersal fish are referred to as white fish.

Herring.

Cod.

FISHING METHODS

Fish have been recognised as a major food source by people around the world from the earliest times. Archaeologists have shown that fishing was important to the first people who settled in Scotland around 7,000 BC.

We can learn about early people from the rubbish they left behind. Remains found in middens at a number of sites show the types of fish exploited. The shells of oysters, mussels, winkles, cockles, whelks and limpets have been found along with the bones of cod, saithe, seals and whales. Despite the tendency of fragile, organic matter like fish bones to decay over time, the number and variety that survive indicate the significance of fish in the Scottish diet.

Tools have also been found which show that three basic methods of catching fish were used: gathering (collecting shellfish from the shore by hand), hunting (actively pursuing fish with hooks and lines, nets or spears) and trapping (luring fish into a trap with or without using bait). Although the technology has developed, these three methods remain the basis of the fishing carried out today.

Fish weir trap.

19th century poaching leister.

Gathering mussels at Fisherrow, East Lothian, 1930s.

EARLY BOATS

As people developed their fishing skills, they looked at ways of exploiting the rich pickings of the open sea. The craft of building and using boats was probably the first and one of the most significant of all technological achievements. Archaeology has shown that Stone Age people used boats and that all boats developed from four basic roots: the raft, the bark boat or canoe (made from a single piece of bark stripped from a tree and stitched together), the skin boat (animal skin or fabric sewn over a wooden frame) and the log boat. Only simple tools were needed to build these boats and they could be adapted for different uses and conditions.

Model salmon coble, based on the traditional skin boat.

Model skin boat or coracle.

Replica logboat and fish weir display.

Methods of Fishing

Early fishermen worked to supply their own needs but we know that fish was traded in Scotland and with Europe from medieval times. It was not until the 18th century, however, that real improvements brought the golden age of sail to Scottish fishing.

The North Sea fishing grounds were commercially exploited from the 14th century by the Dutch using large ships (*busses*). The catch was cured on board each buss to preserve it for the long journey to market. Early attempts to establish a Scottish fishing industry were modelled on this method and in 1766 there were 261 busses in Scotland. Conflict with the Dutch and wars with England and France, however, meant that the fishery was never properly developed.

From the late 18th century, however, a different approach was tried. The Government encouraged fishermen to build small boats and to bring their catch to shore-based curing stations. Smaller boats were less expensive to operate and were perfectly suited to fishing in inshore waters. Real expansion was possible when the end of the Napoleonic Wars in 1815 brought a period of stability and opened up the seas again to peaceful activities. Government bounties and tax relief also encouraged the industry.

Two main ways of fishing were developed to catch the different types of fish: long-lining and drift-netting. As technology and transport links improved, other methods were devised to provide fish for growing urban markets. Fishing became a specialised industry with its own distinctive communities while fishing boats and gear changed as efficiency increased.

CREEL FISHING

Around the coasts of Scotland the catching of lobsters and edible crabs (*partans*) has a long history and is still of considerable importance today. Although other methods are used, the most common is the creel. This is essentially a weighted trap dropped onto the seabed on the end of a long line. It is made of spars of wood (or plastic in recent years) fixed to a base and covered with twine. Entry tunnels lead the crab or lobster into an inner chamber where the bait is placed.

Fishermen mending creels, Dunbar, 1920s.

The creels are collected once or twice per day for the longer they are left, the greater the chance of the catches making their escape (or eating each other!). This is why they are used in inshore waters where the fishermen can make frequent trips to empty them. The boats operating them have to be small enough to work among the rocks and skerries that are the ideal habitat for lobsters and crabs. This has meant the survival of creel-fishing in smaller ports.

Creel fishing is very labour-intensive, but it results in a high quality catch which can attract high prices. Scottish lobster and crab are found on the menus of the most exclusive restaurants and are exported all over the world.

Telfer Thomson at 12 Mid Shore, Buckhaven.

Fishing With Lines

This method, known as long-lining, can be used to catch demersal (white) fish such as cod, halibut, saithe, ling and flatfish. There is evidence of trade in white fish from medieval times, but in 1471 this was still only 10% of the trade in herring or salmon. An exception was Shetland where the white fisheries were the basis of the economy from the 16th century and supplied markets in Europe. Cod in particular was dried and salted for export. The industry became concentrated in the north, east and west coasts providing fish for Edinburgh, Glasgow and Europe.

In the 19th century the industry greatly expanded with boats being used for other purposes such as trade or net fishing in the off-season. Improvements in transport such as railways opened up new markets for fresh fish, while salt cod continued to be exported, particularly to Spain. However, by the 1860s pressure on the mussel beds began to cause problems and in many areas restrictions on bait gathering had to be introduced.

A fisherman tying snoods to a line, c.1900.

Alex Black making a line scull, **by John McGhie RA.**

The advent of steam trawling in the 1880s finally caused the decline of lining, as the markets were flooded with cheap fish. Despite the labour required, long-lining did continue in some areas, particularly Gourdon, into the late 20th century. Two principal methods were employed:

Sma' Lines

Small line fishing was a family affair with women and children responsible for much of the work in preparing the equipment. This was a line, up to a mile in length, to which were attached *snoods* or shorter pieces of line. Each snood had a hook which was baited with fish or shellfish. The woman's work started in the early morning when she would go down to the shore to gather mussels. Then she would shell these and put one on each hook. There were around 1,200 hooks per line and each fisherman had two lines. The lines were neatly coiled in a *scull* (basket) and layered with grass (gathered by the children) to prevent them snagging as they were shot out. It was not uncommon

for a woman to work a ten hour day to prepare her husband or father's gear for a single trip. Sma' lining would be done in inshore waters in the winter between herring or great lines seasons.

Preparing the lines at North Street, St.Andrews.

Baiting the lines, Elie, late 1800s.

Digging up lugworms for bait, Pittenweem, 1895.

GARTLINS

Hauling gartlins amid Arctic ice on an Aberdeen steam liner.

Great line (*gartlin*) fishing was similar to small line fishing but was undertaken in deeper waters, further out to sea. The lines could be up to fifteen miles in length and would be fitted with 5,000 hooks. The fishermen usually baited the lines on the boat. Many liners carried a small-meshed drift net to catch young herring to use as bait, or would buy small haddock from other fishermen. The main grounds were very distant, for example the Faroe Banks north of Shetland, so the men could be out at sea for three weeks at a time.

Equipment was developed to try to make the work of shooting and hauling the lines easier. A metal tube or sleeve prevented the hooks snagging in the fishermen's skin or clothing as the line was shot at speed over its surface. A mechanical or steam-powered winch or line-hauler (named *Irnman* in the Forth area) was used to pull in the lines. As the line came in, the fish were grabbed using a hook tied to a pole. They were gutted on board and the livers saved in barrels to make cod liver oil.

Jackie Taylor of the *Brighter Hope II* with a halibut, 1955.

SHETLAND HAAF FISHING

The seas around Shetland abounded with fish, far exceeding the supplies needed by the islands' population. Therefore the surplus was traded with mainland Britain and Europe. From the 1720s, local landowners systematically developed the fisheries, and tenants were often forced to pay part of their rent in fish. This system, known as fishing tenure was also found on the West coast. As the population and the pressure on the land increased, fishing grew in importance as it was the only way the people of Shetland could support themselves.

The fishermen would go far out to sea (haaf is the Norse word for ocean), perhaps twice a week, with six or seven miles of line per trip. The catch was mainly cod and ling and by the 18th century Shetland was producing 80% of the white fish exported from Britain. The fish were split and salted by the old men and boys before being laid out to dry on the shingle beaches. During the two-month summer season, the workers lived in huts at haaf stations, as close as possible to the fishing grounds.

INTERIOR SHETLAND CROFTERS COTTAGE.

PHOTO BY RAMSAY LERWICK

Cod drying on the beach prior to export, Shetland, _c._1900.

Fishing With Nets

Nets can be used in inshore waters, operated either from the shore, from boats or fixed to poles to trap fish. More extensively they are also used in open water to catch pelagic fish (such as herring, mackerel and sprats) that swim in shoals near the surface of the sea. The nets are expensive to maintain but the fishermen can be rewarded with bumper catches.

FIXED NETS

These are used primarily in inshore waters and near estuaries up and down the coast to catch salmon. Strips of netting are set on the shore at low tide in shallow water to form an enclosure with an opening facing towards the beach. The fish swim in towards the shore with the incoming tide and are then trapped by the nets as the tide recedes. In all cases the net is heavy enough to guide or hold rather than to enmesh the fish.

The various designs that were developed include bag nets, stake or fly nets, and jumper nets. Salmon was commonly sought in the Solway, Tweed and around Montrose. There are now very few fishers of wild salmon left owing to the competition from cheaper, farmed fish pricing them out of the market.

Harvesting salmon nets.   **Stake nets at Montrose.**

DRIFT-NETTING

Hauling herring aboard the *Refleurir* KY16.

Herring, the most significant pelagic fish, was important to the Scottish economy from medieval times but Scottish fishermen lagged behind the Dutch in developing the industry. At first they used inshore, fixed nets but from the early 18th century drift nets were used in deeper waters. The Forth was the first area to use larger boats with crews of seven or eight men, some of whom might be farmers drafted in for the season.

A drift net hangs in the water like a curtain and catches the fish by the gills as they swim through it. Cork floats at the top and weights at the bottom keep it upright. In the past a number of nets could be strung together on a messenger rope. Latterly the weight of manilla rope was enough to keep the net vertical and sinkers were dispensed with. Larger floats made of bladders or skins lined with tar marked the joints in the nets. In 1884, Alex Black of Cellardyke invented canvas buoys or *pallets* to replace these.

Hauling drift nets on the *Royal Sovereign* KY75, 1930s.

A good catch of herring in the nets at Peterhead.

The boats would sail in the evening, reaching the fishing grounds as darkness fell. The nets were shot out and the boat would drift with them. Herring usually rose to the surface to feed through the night and, if they encountered the net, would be entangled in it. At dawn, the work of hauling in the nets began. The fish were shaken out into the hold as they came over the side. This could take many hours, depending on the size of the catch and the number of nets. Then the boat had to turn for home, rushing the fresh catch to port.

Tradition has it that Fife fishermen brought the technique of drift-netting to the Moray Firth before 1700 and established a fishery there. The Clyde fishery also developed from the 17th century as there were more reliable herring stocks in sheltered waters and a ready market in Ireland.

John Reid preparing canvas buoys.

Mending nets aboard the *Winaway* KY279, 1942.

By 1800, herring dominated Scottish fishing and the industry continued to develop throughout the next century. In 1800 around 50,000 barrels of cured herring were produced. By the 1880s this had risen to over a million, reaching a peak of over two million around 1910. Even in the early days, a boat could catch as much as 50 crans (one cran is around 1,000 herring) in one trip, although it was rare until the 1860s for a boat to take 200 crans in a season.

The industry was increasingly regulated resulting in higher quality products that were in demand across Europe. Improvements in gear also contributed: in the early 19th century home-made nets of linen or hemp were used and each boat carried up to twelve. In the 1860s, cotton was introduced which was weaker but lighter so boats could carry more nets. By the 1890s the largest boats were shooting over 70 nets (up to two miles in total length). In the later 19th century, however, new and more efficient ways of using nets became inceasingly dominant.

The crew of the *Cosmea* KY21 boiling the nets in alum.

TRAWLING

A trawl net is dragged along the seabed behind a boat and scoops up the fish in its path. There is evidence of an early form of trawling in England from the 14th century and the practice was regulated from the 1630s when concerns were raised about mesh sizes. Trawling was more widely used in England from the early 19th century but was was not known in Scotland until the 1860s. Some fishermen, mainly around Buckhaven, took up the beam trawl method to catch white fish such as haddock and cod as an alternative to line fishing. The net was formed from a mesh bag with the mouth held open by a beam or a box-like arrangement.

Steam trawler *Nellie Nutton* GN69.

This method resulted in large catches. However, the fish were of poorer quality than line-caught fish as they could be crushed and there was little selection. The method did not become widely popular until steam power solved the problem of keeping a steady speed while hauling the trawl. Even in its early forms, however, trawling caused considerable controversy as line fishermen accused trawlers of taking fish that were too small, of destroying the ground and of damaging their gear at sea.

In more recent years, developments in gear and technology have allowed trawlers to be more selective and to fish at different depths so that trawling has been successfully adapted to shellfish and to pelagic fishing.

RING-NETTING

Ring-netting developed in the sheltered waters around Loch Fyne in Argyll. The Clyde had developed into a successful fishing area supplying the urban centres of Glasgow and Strathclyde with fish caught locally and around the Northern Isles. Large-scale drift-netting was not suited to the confined waters of the lochs so ring-netting, firstly shore-based, then operated by two boats working together, was developed in the mid 19th century.

Ring-netter *Boy Danny* CN142 at St. Monans, 1948.

The method involves surrounding a shoal of fish with a net and then pulling the ring tight to trap them. The two boats would sail to the fishing ground where one would remain at a certain point with one end of the net. The other would sail round in a circle, shooting the net as it went, until it rejoined the first boat. Both crews would then board one vessel to haul in the nets.

This was cheaper and more efficient than drift-netting but concerns over the effects on fish stocks were raised from the beginning. Following conflict with other fishermen, the method was banned in 1851. The ban was largely ignored and was lifted in 1867, from which time ring-netting dominated the Clyde and spread to other sheltered waters such as the Forth.

SEINE NETTING

The seine net originated in Denmark but it was not used in Scotland until the early 1920s. After the collapse of the herring markets in 1914 many fishermen were looking for other sources of income to see them through the summer months. Seining was an attractive alternative.

The seine net is a drag net used to catch whitefish. The net mouth is kept open by weights at the bottom and floats at the top. Long ropes are attached to wings at either side of the mouth. The boat completes a triangular course, shooting one of these ropes, attached to an anchored marker buoy (*dahn*), followed by the net and finally the second rope. The boat returns to the dahn leaving the open net behind it. The vessel hauls both ropes in together, closing the net around the fish.

Rope reels aboard the *Harmony* INS257.

Boats from Moray and north east Scotland were the first to adopt the method. Seine-netting was profitable and saved the hard work of baiting lines. Purpose-built seiners were developed with deck machinery such as a powerful seine net winch invented by C Paterson of Macduff. This equipment was relatively cheap to buy and encouraged many fishermen to take up the new method.

PURSE-SEINING

Purse-seiner *Zephyr* LK394 of Whalsay, Shetland, 1982.

Purse-seining was introduced into Great Britain in 1966. After a slow start, the number of purse-seiners steadily increased until the purse-seine net became the principal method used to catch pelagic fish, until superseded by mid-water trawling,.

The nets are lightweight synthetic material and work on the principle of a drawstring purse. A net is set to form a wall of webbing surrounding the fish, the top of the net lying on, or just below, the surface. When the net has circled the shoal, its bottom is drawn together forming a bag. The fish are gathered alongside the vessel and are then hoisted aboard. The purse-seine net is enormous, and can enclose a volume of water the size of St. Paul's Cathedral.

From 1967 to the 1990s, purse-seine boats (pursers) were made of steel, gradually increasing in size from 80 feet to 200 feet long (24.4 – 61 metres). They were very versatile and could be adapted for pair trawling for herring, sand-eel, cod or mackerel making them viable all year round. Most had a crew of twelve to fifteen. Purse-seiners could catch huge quantities of fish and at least 1100 tons of fish could be held in their refrigerated tanks. These catches were mainly for human consumption and also for processing into meal and animal feed.

The Fishing Fleet

The shape of a boat is dictated by two main concerns: the need to stay afloat and the need to control the boat's movement. From the earliest times, vessels had to be robust and seaworthy to operate from Scotland's exposed coasts. However, the designs were the product of many generations of modification and there was considerable regional variation. Local conditions, the method of fishing preferred, tradition and outside influences all played a part in shaping the distinctive characters of the boats.

Rowing a salmon coble, Montrose.

Walter Reekie boatbuilders, St. Monans, 1946.

Early fishermen, catching only enough fish to supply their own needs, used small boats, up to 20 feet (six metres) in length powered by oars or a square sail on a single mast. They were clinker built and undecked. The size was limited by the number of men available to crew the boats and by the daily need to pull them up onto the beach before the widespread development of harbours.

The building of such craft was also a local affair with many fishermen building their own boats. Skills and techniques were passed down the generations and designs perfected by master craftsmen. As fishing became a commercial industry, boat-building remained a central feature of fishing communities and most harbours would boast at least one boat-building firm employed in building and repairing vessels. Some of these became famous and produced boats that were sold across the world. Only in the 20th century did iron and steel boat-building come to dominate.

THE DAYS OF SAIL

Fraserburgh Harbour, *c*.1900.

Sails were used from ancient times to capture the power of the wind. Various ways of rigging evolved as fishermen sought how best to manage this force to their own advantage and specific needs.

Fifies heading out to sea.

The traditional rig in Northern waters was a square sail set on a single mast. This design was known in Ancient Egypt, on Viking longships, on medieval vessels and persists today in the Fair Isle skiff. It developed into the lug rig, which was to dominate the Scottish east coast throughout the 19th century. The large four-sided lug sails provided great speed but had to be lowered (dipped) and passed around the mast to change direction. The sails and masts were also lowered while fishing to prevent the boat rolling. This was such hard work that the lug rig was only an advantage in open waters offshore and needed a large crew, such as that required on a fishing boat, to handle it.

A smaller mizzen sail was used for manoeuvring and could be used for making small movements while at nets. By varying the number of sails hoisted and the amount canvas opened out, fishermen could suit their sails to the weather conditions or activity.

Although there were many local variations in Scottish boat design, there were a number of main types which can be identified. Captain John Washington detailed some in a report in 1848. Smaller versions of the large vessels are known in Scotland as yawls or yoles, the word meaning small boat.

Sailing boats reached the peak of their development in the 1880s and 90s and some continued to hold their own after the introduction of steamers. New gear was introduced to help with hauling lines and nets and handling masts and sails (which by the 1890s could weigh two or three tons). One Zulu, *Muirneag*, carried on fishing, powered by sails alone, until 1946.

Research LK828 with typical Shetland smack rig.

These vessels were developed in Orkney and Shetland and used mainly in Northern fishing waters. The boats were pointed at both the bow and stern (known as double-ended), and raked both fore and aft. This was reminiscent of the long historical connections of Orkney with the Vikings, indeed many boats were imported in kit form from Norway, there being a shortage of timber in Orkney and Shetland.

The main variations were a sixern, fourern and yole, the design being largely identical in each save for the overall size. A sixern which, as the name suggests, was powered by six oars, was the largest and quite capable of handling the open North Sea and Atlantic. The yole was a smaller boat used for inshore fishing amongst the voes and skerries of the islands. The flexible, light build made them excellent craft at riding the waves and bending with the forces of the water. Their simple rigging and square sail took great skill to operate.

Boats of the East Coast

Scaffie

From Wick to the southern shores of the Moray Firth, the Scaffie was favoured. These boats measured 20 to 40 feet (approximately 6 to 12 metres) in length and had a curved stem and forefoot, and a very sharply raked stern. This made the keel relatively short and allowed the boats to turn easily in narrow waterways. Normally they were rigged with one or two masts (even three on the largest vessels), with lug sails. They were very light so that they could be beached easily by their five-man crew. They had a larger area of working space on board for their size but they lacked the Fifie's ability to run with the wind.

Scaffies landing their catch, near Invergordon, *c*.1905.

Fifie

Between Aberdeen and Eyemouth, the more heavily built Fifie was most commonly used. The stem and the stern were almost vertical and the tendency was to build them larger than Scaffies, measuring 65 feet (20 metres) or more in overall length. They had a long straight keel and this made them fast, but not as manoeuvrable as the Scaffie. The Fifies had two masts. They used a dipping lug on the fore-mast and a standing lug on the mizzen. Although this rig was simple, fishermen needed great skill to use it safely. In Shetland, the smack (gaff) rig was preferred as it was easier to handle in restricted waters where frequent turning was required.

Neither Fifies nor Scaffies were decked until 1885, it having been considered that fishing boats should be open. However, due to the persistence and example of the RNLI who built and tested a partly-decked boat, fishermen were eventually persuaded to convert to boats which were decked and, therefore, much safer in heavy weather.

A Zulu (left) and a Fifie (right).

Zulu

The Zulu type of fishing boat was introduced by William Campbell of Lossiemouth in 1879 with his vessel *Nonesuch*. The vessel was an attempt to combine the best features of both the Fifie and Scaffie and had a vertical stem and raked stern.

The Zulu (so called because of the Zulu Wars raging at the time of its invention) was an immediate success and quickly came to dominate the north east coast fleet. There were continued developments of the design: steering wheels replaced the traditional tillers in around 1895 and steam-powered capstans were introduced in the 1880s. The latter took over from hand-powered winches, allowing a greater weight of sail to be handled, and so led to the building of bigger boats.

At their peak, Zulus could reach 80 feet (24.4 metres) in length. The mast was as long as the keel and the boat would be crewed by seven or eight men and a boy. Commercially it was fast, giving a speedy return to port with catches which exceeded the capacities of either the Fifie or the Scaffie.

Boats of the West Coast

Loch Fyne Skiff

These boats were developed in the 1880s to pursue the ring-netting in Loch Fyne. They were around 30 feet (9.1 metres) long with a near vertical stem and sharply raked, pointed stern. A deck provided some shelter for the crew and allowed the boat to sail on longer trips. They were considerably deeper at the aft end of the keel than at the bow and this made for a very handy vessel which could turn tightly. This was ideal for casting the ring net in its characteristic circle.

Sgoth

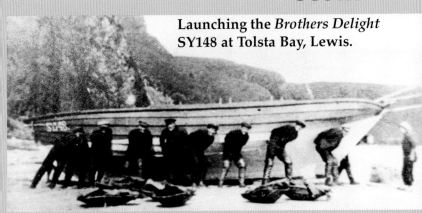

Launching the *Brothers Delight* SY148 at Tolsta Bay, Lewis.

The Sgoth (pronounced *skaw*) was a line-fishing vessel of around 25 feet (7.7 metres) in length built on the Isle of Lewis for working the exposed and dangerous seas around the Outer Hebrides. These specialised craft had to be able to manoeuvre in the restricted waters around the islands and also to withstand the pounding waves of the open Atlantic Ocean.

The Sgoth is more strongly framed than boats of the Northern Isles and has the rounded stern typical of boats of the Western Isles. This shape was difficult to build but gave plenty of buoyancy. Sgoths were often beach-launched and were rigged with a dipping lugsail.

Loch Fyne skiffs at Tarbert, *c*.1905.

THE AGE OF STEAM

The design of sailing boats continued to be developed and refined throughout the 1800s. However, the efficiency of these vessels was still dependent on an uncontrollable factor, the power of the wind.

Steam drifter *Honeydew* BF122 leaving Fraserburgh, 1940s.

The mid 19th century saw a breakthrough when steam-powered marine engines, powered by coal from Scotland's large reserves in Fife and the Lothians, were developed. After experimentation with steam power for trawling in the 1870s, Scotland's first purpose-built steam trawler was built in Leith in 1882. She was the *Hawk* and, like all early steam trawlers, was fully rigged for sail in case the machinery broke down. Local fishermen were impressed and more boats were ordered, most bought from Hull and fitted out at Granton.

However, they were expensive to buy (at £3,500 over twice the cost of a sailing boat, rising to £10,000 in the 1890s when iron hulls replaced wood), and to run. This deterred many individual skippers from switching to steam and led to the practice of company ownership. The bigger trawler owners established fleets near to the large cities that could supply the capital, labour, transport and markets required. Edinburgh (with its deep water harbours of Leith and Granton) and Aberdeen became the Scottish trawling centres.

Right: **Steam drifter *Hero* INS209 on war service.**

Many of the steam vessels built before 1900 were built as line vessels. However, the higher operating costs associated with steam (including fuel and two extra crew to tend the engine and boiler) meant that they could not afford to fish at the lines all year round. Many were sold on or converted for drifting. A few remained at Aberdeen, occasionally landing at South Shields. Some Cellardyke men continued at the lines, combining it with the Forth winter herring season.

Drifters were not so dependent on a steady wind as trawlers and usually fished closer to shore. Therefore they were slow to switch to steam power because the cost of vessels and fuel seemed to outweigh any benefits. Two steam boats worked drift nets out of Wick in 1880 and did no better than their sailing counterparts, at higher cost. 1897, however, saw the launch of the *Consolation LT718*, regarded as the first steam vessel built purely for drifting, and the era of the steam drifter had begun.

By 1910, Scottish yards were following their English counterparts in producing large numbers of wooden-hulled steam drifters, powered by compound engines. The introduction of iron or steel-hulled vessels led to even larger boats; many (the so-called *standard* drifters) built by the Admiralty during and after the First World War. However, because of their size (up to 100 feet/30.4 metres in length), they were confined to to the larger ports. Increasing engine efficiency and cheap coal made the steam vessels competitive and they contributed to the bumper catches around 1913. However, even at their peak, sailing vessels at top speed could outrun them, and were easier to convert to motor power when this was introduced. The last steam drifter, the *Wilson Line*, was launched in Aberdeen in 1932.

Steam drifter *Baden Powell* SN286 by G Wade, *c*.1910.

Scottish steam drifters heading into Yarmouth.

Trawler *The Bruce* LH21 taking on coal at Granton.

Long-liner *Radiation* A115 built at Anstruther in 1957.

Even as steam power was taking a hold on the Scottish fleet, experiments with diesel and petrol powered engines paved the way for motorised fishing vessels (MFVs). The internal combustion engine was invented in the late 19th century. In 1895, it was first used to propel a Danish fishing boat and, after trials in Scotland in 1905, was quickly adopted here. Sailing boats were relatively easy to convert: the engines were comparatively small and, unlike steam engines, did not require bulky fuel or extra crew to operate.

Eyemouth skippers were among the first in Scotland to install engines. World War I spurred technological development and many of the old sailing Fifies were converted in this way. The number of motor boats in the Scottish fleet overtook that of steam boats in 1915. A further spur was the coal dispute of 1921 which boosted demand for motor boats as coal prices soared.

The Engine that is driving
470 FISHING BOATS
in the United Kingdom alone.
6 TO 60 H.P.

PETROL OR PARAFFIN.

KELVIN

Manufacturers—
THE BERGIUS LAUNCH & ENGINE CO.
DOBBIES LOAN, GLASGOW.

Motor liner *Verbena* KY97.

Hauling lines on the *Ocean Sceptre* KY378, 1983.

The increasing power and efficiency of marine engines brought changes both to the methods of fishing and to the design of boats. Boat hulls moved away from sailing boat designs, as they were no longer dependent on the forces of nature to carry them across the sea but could force their way through. West coast ring-netters and the early seine-netters of the Moray Firth were the first to break with tradition and new boat designs were introduced from the 1920s when a more rounded cruiser stern began to replace the narrow Fifie style.

War again acted as a spur to development from 1939 - 45 and the Admiralty again built boats that were turned over to the fishermen when hostilities ceased. Grants and loans stimulated a post-war building boom with the need for maximum power and maximum volume as the main driving forces. Since then, there has been a revolution in design. From the 1960s, hull shapes began to fill out and boats became shorter, wider and rounder. From the 1970s, the square transom stern became common as it gave more room on deck for the crew and for the increasingly powerful hydraulic power blocks and winches used to haul in the nets.

More thought was given to the safety and comfort of the crew and, increasingly, shelters were built to protect the men working on board. These could take the form of a *whaleback* giving a covered area at the bow, to a partial or full aluminium *shelter deck* enclosing the deck and wheelhouse. On such boats the nets are operated through hatches and the men are completely protected from the elements. This enables them to venture out in almost all weathers. However, the sea is still dangerous and boats are now subject to strict safety testing and must carry a range of safety equipment.

The steady pulling power of an engine increased the potential for using trawl-type nets to scoop up fish. Seine-netters, following the Danish model, pursers and trawlers of all types became increasingly dominant. New materials made boats and gear more durable and more able to venture further from shore. Motor power has been applied to almost every aspect of fishing until now modern vessels with their hydraulic winches, refrigeration units and powerful engines are unrecognisable in comparison with their counterparts of 100 years ago.

Even smaller vessels have benefited from engine power and today the fastest growing section of the fleet is the "under 10 metres" category used mainly for trawling and dredging inshore waters for prawns and other shellfish. Pretty shapes have been sacrificed for efficiency and safety, and modern fishing boats are designed chiefly to be working platforms, able to carry big engines and big catches.

The *Golden Splendour* INS63, built in 1973.   Seiner *Dalriada* BF262.

NAVIGATION AND FISH-FINDING

Once out at sea, fishermen need to know where they are and where to find the fish. Over the centuries, fishermen have not been slow to take advantage of scientific developments that have brought improvements in equipment that could be used for navigation and fish-finding.

Traditionally, inshore fishermen would navigate using landmarks along the coast and their local knowledge of currents and tides. They also had a sounding lead, a weighted line that they could lower over the side to measure the depth of the water. A piece of tallow was stuck to the bottom of the weight and the sediment that stuck to it (sand, shingle or mud) provided another clue.

Offshore, early fishermen had to rely on a magnetic compass and the sun and stars. Instruments were invented which used the angle of the sun above the horizon to measure latitude. Longitude was more difficult to measure and could not be reliably calculated until the invention of an accurate clock. A log was used to measure the boat's speed over a certain time and so calculate the distance travelled. The first chart was produced for the North Sea in the 17th century and these became increasingly relied upon for determining position.

Fish-finding was another skill fishermen required as shoals moved from place to place and there was no guarantee of returning home with a good catch. Observation of the water (oily patches on the surface could indicate a shoal) or the behaviour of seabirds were the first methods used, along with local knowledge. The feeling wire was an early mechanical device to help locate shoals, however, it was not until the invention of radar and echo-sounding in the 20th century that fish-finding became more precise.

The Scottish fishing industry has changed dramatically since the 1940s and 50s. New technology, much of it initially developed for military use, has made boats and fishing gear more efficient so that fewer men and boats can catch many more fish. Technology has revolutionised the following areas:

NAVIGATION

From the 1950s, the compass and chart were supplemented by radar, which enabled the boats to navigate at night when landmarks could not be seen, and other radio navigation methods. The most well known of these was the Decca system which used co-ordinated radio beams picked up by a Decca Receiver and a special chart to pinpoint the boat's location. These have now been superseded by GPS systems which use signals from orbiting satellites to fix the boat's position.

Navigation has traditionally been the role of the boat's skipper who often worked alone in the wheelhouse. It was not uncommon for the crew to be ignorant of their exact position, so closely did the skipper guard his secrets of where to find the best fishing grounds.

One of the museum's large collection of fishing boat electronics.

COMMUNICATION

Although the fishermen still have to use the visual signals developed by earlier generations (such as flags and lights arranged to show when the boat is fishing etc.), radio communication has become increasingly important. Boats can talk to each other, and to the agents and officials in port to let them know how the fishing trip is going and when they will be back with their catch.

One of the most important uses of the radio is to transmit and receive distress messages if a boat gets into trouble so that help can be summoned quickly.

Inside the wheelhouse of the *Ocean Quest*.

FISH-FINDING

Although originally developed as a navigation tool (to map the seabed beneath the boat and so indicate its position) sonar and the echo-sounder soon proved invaluable aids to finding fish. Both use similar equipment to transmit and receive sound waves through the water. The echo-sounder points its beam vertically down while the sonar is used horizontally to sweep the sea around the boat. Shoals are recorded on the receiver, showing the fishermen where to shoot their lines or nets.

These innovations have made fishing more and more efficient and have contributed to the fast pace of change. Wheelhouses have grown bigger to accommodate all the electronic equipment now carried. From his wheelhouse chair, the skipper knows exactly where he is, where his fishing gear is and what type and where the fish are. Improvements in navigation, communication and fish-finding equipment have vastly increased fishing efficiency.

Atlas echo-sounder.

REGULATION AND ENVIRONMENTAL CONCERNS

Fishery regulation is nothing new: there were restrictions on fishing in medieval times, especially relating to salmon, and to herring. From the first, these rules had the twin (and in some cases, conflicting) aims of conserving fish stocks while maximising the earnings from the industry.

The power for imposing regulations passed from local landowners and the Crown to the Government (through the Fishery Board set up in the early 19th century) and then on to the EEC and EU. Regulation has increased in parallel with developments in fishing gear and technology. Restrictions could be placed on new types of fishing gear, mesh sizes of nets, fishing areas and seasons, and total allowable catches and quotas. Concern over declining fish stocks (particularly of demersal fish) have added to the impetus and stringency of restrictions from the later 20th century.

The 1950s - 70s saw the episodes known as the Cod Wars where British boats clashed with Icelandic vessels after Iceland extended its territorial waters and designated them an exclusive zone only to be fished by Icelandic boats. This barred many Scottish trawlers from their habitual fishing grounds and tensions boiled over into violence on a number of occasions. In 1958, 1972-3 and 1975-6 the Royal Navy took action to protect British fishing vessels in the North Atlantic while Icelandic vessels defended their new waters. Eventually agreement was reached under international law whereby Britain accepted the increased territorial limits in return for a catch allowance.

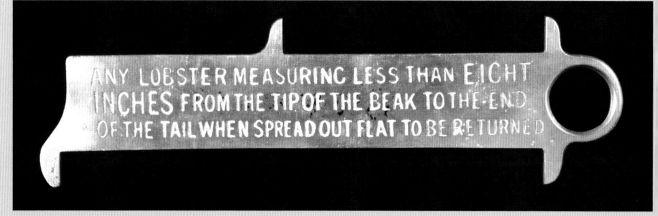

Gauge for measuring crabs and lobsters.

Undersized fish rejected by inspectors.

In recent years the EEC, followed by the EU, has played an ever more dominant role in controlling catches. The struggle to balance marine conservation, environmental issues, the economic viability of the industry, and the needs of fishing communities has become increasingly intense. Severe cuts in quotas and days allowed at sea have resulted in huge reductions in Scottish fishing fleets as fishermen struggle to survive financially within the current framework. More recently, selective fishing gear has been developed to ensure that only target species are caught. Fisheries research is ongoing and it is yet to be seen whether the stringent measures have allowed stocks to recover as planned. Meanwhile, many fishing harbours and communities have been altered beyond all recognition.

HERRING FISHERY.

WHEREAS, notwithſtanding repeated Intimation has been given, that the Indulgence hitherto granted with regard to the Size of the Meſhes of Nets was to ceaſe at the Expiration of the preſent Fiſhing Seaſon, and that the Law, in that reſpect, would thereafter be fully enforced; an expectation is ſtill entertained by Fiſhermen and others that ſuch indulgence will be ſtill further continued: The Commiſſioners for the Herring Fiſhery hereby again give public notice, that from and after the 5th day of April 1811, no Net ſhall be uſed for the purpoſe of catching Herrings, the Meſhes whereof are leſs than One Inch from Knot to Knot, otherwiſe the ſame ſhall be ſeized, and the Owner thereof proſecuted according to Law. And to the end that no Perſon may plead Ignorance of what the Law is, a Copy of the 12th Section of the Act 48 Geo. III. Cap. 110. is hereto ſubjoined.

Section 12.—" And be it further enacted, That from and after
" the firſt day of June One thouſand eight hundred and nine, no
" Perſon ſhall uſe in any River or Loch, or at Sea, in or on the Coaſt
" of Great Britain, any Herring Net, or any Traul Net, Drag Net, or
" other Sea Net, for the taking of Herrings, which hath a Meſh of
" leſs than One Inch from Knot to Knot, or any falſe or double
" Bottom, Cod, or Pouch, or ſhall put any Net, though of legal ſize,
" behind the others to deſtroy the ſmall Fiſh; and that every Perſon
" offending herein ſhall forfeit every ſuch Net as aforeſaid, and the ſum
" of Forty Pounds for every ſuch Offence; and it ſhall be lawful for
" the Commiſſioners for the Herring Fiſhery, to be appointed pur-
" ſuant to this Act, to cauſe every ſuch Net to be burnt."

By Order of the Commiſſioners,

JA^s DUNSMURE, *Sec*.

Office for the Herring Fiſhery,
Edinburgh, 22d January 1811.

Herring Fishery Act, 1811.

Fisherfolk and Communities

Fishermen's houses at Crovie.

Fisherfolk have long been regarded, and have regarded themselves, as a race apart. As the fishing industry became more specialised, along with it developed a distinctive community of fisherfolk with its own character and traditions.

Medieval fishermen lived on the outskirts of towns but in time, they began to live in smaller villages close to the sheltered bays or beaches they used as harbours. In the 17th century, a number of landowners created planned fishing villages. These were not all successful but some, such as Tarbert, persist to this day. However, the tradition of the crofter-fisherman continued on much of the West coast. On the East coast the building of harbours and ever-larger fishing boats increasingly focused fishing on fewer main ports. There the fishing communities had their own distinct areas: either within a town or in a separate village they were a people apart.

Fishing was a community effort. Families banded together to buy and operate boats and everyone was involved in preparing and maintaining the gear. It was not uncommon for women to own shares in boats and traditionally the women had control of any earnings. From the 19th century women also travelled with the fleets to work in the curing stations as herring lasses, which gave them a certain amount of independence and freedom. Both men and women spent long periods away from their homes and families, especially after the season was extended to include Yarmouth.

Drying nets from *gallowses*, Buckhaven, *c.*1910.

LIFE ON BOARD:
BOAT OWNERSHIP

In Scotland, fishing boats were usually owned by the fishermen themselves and only rarely by shore-based companies. This meant that the fishermen themselves reaped the rewards of a good season, or bore the risk of a poor one.

Sometimes a businessman or shopkeeper might put up the money for shares in a boat but more often it was groups of fishermen and their families. Even with the increased catching power of steam or motor boats, earnings were erratic and the few shore-based companies that were set up lasted only a few years. The exceptions were fish salesmen. A number became significant sources of funding. For example, R Irvin & Sons of North Shields had shares in many drifters from Buckie, Hopeman and Burghead while in Macduff, A Peterson & Co. was the main shareholder.

The boats were generally sold in 32 shares, and young men would buy perhaps four, hoping to get more later. Occasionally an older retiring skipper might sell his boat but keep four or eight shares; parting with a boat was almost like a death in the family.

A share system was also used on board for the supply of gear (nets, ropes, buoys etc.). For example, the seven deck-workers on the steam drifters each provided nets: seven for the winter herring fishing, thirteen for the summer off the northeast coast and eleven for the East Anglian season. They would have the same again as spares.

Earnings were divided equally into three between the men (further divided between the seven deckhands and the cook who each got an equal share); the gear (divided amongst those who supplied gear); and the boat (divided amongst the owners depending on how many shares they owned).

Sometimes a man might fish as a *half-deal's man* (he supplied no gear), so his gear share would go to whoever made up the shortfall. Only the engineer and fireman were paid a wage. Expenses were always paid first before the *pairtin'* of the earnings.

Sandy Wood of Pittenweem, *c*.1880

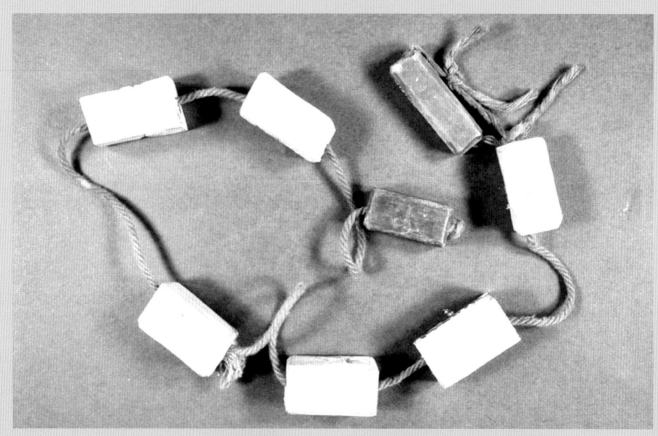

Pirns, marked with their owner's initials and tied to fishing gear.

Fifie *Vanguard* KY603 at Anstruther.

Boat Names

A fisherman's fate is bound up with his vessel so the naming of a fishing boat is taken very seriously. Names can be religious, traditional, poetic or humorous but always significant:

FAMILY NAMES

Many boats are named after members of the owner's family – often a mother, wife or daughter. Sometimes, this indicated that the person has a share in the boat's ownership. Occasionally, family names can be used to create a totally new word – for example the Pittenweem boat *Wilsheernie* was named after Wilma, Sheila and Ernie Wood. The *Nostaw* of Campbeltown was taken from the then owner's name (Watson) spelled backwards.

COMPANY NAMES

Groups of fishermen or companies with a fleet of boats (usually trawlers) often give them similar names. For example, the *Scarlet Cord*, *Thread and Line* of G T Buchanan, Port Seton; the *Granton Falcon*, *Harrier*, *Merlin* and *Osprey* of British United Trawlers (Scotland), Granton; *Admiral Burnett*, *Drake*, *Hawke* and *Jellicoe* of Parbel-Smith Ltd., Aberdeen; and *Kelso*, *Duff*, *Barbara*, *Finlay*, *Gregor* and *Elizabeth Paton* of the Ardrossan Trawling Co., Glasgow.

BIBLICAL NAMES

These are less common now than in the days of sail when the fishermen were more at the mercy of the elements. Many could be related to the beliefs of the owner. Others (e.g. *Brighter Hope*, *Fruitful Bough*, *Lively Hope*, *Harvest Gleaner*) combine a Biblical reference with a more materialistic hope for a good catch. Still others (e.g. *Mizpah*, *Chrysolite*, *Nimrod*, *True Vine*) are more obscure and have probably persisted because they have become traditional in a family as "lucky" boats. Others such as *Crystal Tide* and *Morning Star* reflect the fisherman's experience of being at sea and have probably lost their direct Biblical connotations.

Prawn trawler *Nimrod III* KY79 off Pittenweem.

Crew of the steam drifter *Pursuit* KY152, *c*.1910.

NAMES FROM MYTHOLOGY AND HISTORY

Names such as *Hercules, Golden Fleece, Valkyrie* and *Amalthea* are taken from Roman, Greek and Norse myth and legend. Some names are taken from famous historic ships or people e.g. *Taeping, Cutty Sark, Mayflower, Chaucer, Churchill* and *Flora MacDonald.*

OTHER LANGUAGES

Latin names give an air of class and usually express the hopes of the fisherman or his faith in his boat e.g. *Inter Nos* (Between Us), *Nulli Secundus* (Second to None), *Spes Bona* (Good Hope). Gaelic names are more common on the west coast and reflect the same themes as other names e.g. *Sireadh* (Seeking), *Lub Dhubh* (Black Bay), *Reul na Maidne* (Morning Star). Sometimes boats built elsewhere keep their names e.g. *Solstrale* (Norwegian for Sunbeam).

ADMIRALTY "STANDARD" NAMES

Standard drifters and trawlers built by the Admiralty during World War I were named after the elements e.g. *Afterglow, Blizzard, Radiation, White Horses, Lasher, Galaxy,* and *Nimbus.* Some kept their names when transferred to the fishing fleet and occasionally these names (such as *Radiation*) remained popular and were used for later boats.

THE CREW

Small boats used for inshore fishing could be crewed by a single man or two working together. The larger sailing vessels usually had a crew of seven, including a young boy who was there to literally "learn the ropes" while serving as cook. Most steam vessels carried a crew of ten. Besides controlling the boat, fishing, and looking after the gear, some had specific jobs on board.

THE SKIPPER

He was in charge of the vessel and had the final say on any decisions. He had to hold a Board of Trade Certificate or *Skipper's Ticket* signifying that he had passed examinations on navigation, marine regulations and law. A skipper had to be over 21 years old.

THE MATE

He was second-in-command and held a *Mate's Ticket*.

FIVE DECKHANDS

They required no tickets but many had them, ready for future use.

THE COOK

A boy invariably started his career, aged around 14, as a cook and coiler, usually on a boat where his father was a crew-member and could watch over the lad. On a steam drifter, a heavy, tarred, leader rope connected the nets. This had to be coiled into a box below decks as the nets were hauled in. This was the cook's job and took at least three hours. Immediately the nets were hauled, the cook had to get the breakfast ready. He was responsible for all meals on board, while picking up fishing skills from the others.

John Watson *English Jock* of Crail.

Skipper's certificate of John Wood, 1933.

An engineer and a fireman tended the engine and boiler. Although protected from the elements, they had their own struggles to avoid being thrown against the furnace or moving machinery as the boat tossed in a swell. They did not need to have any qualifications but a very few did. They were known as the *black squad* and were paid a weekly wage, rather than a share of the profits. In the 1920s and 30s it averaged around £3 per week for an engineer and £2 10/- for a fireman. They could make extra money when on watch by catching fish by hand-line. The fish were marked and sold separately and the money kept as a bonus known as *stoker*.

Chief Engineer's certificate of Alexander McRonald, 1931.

Cellardyke fishermen wearing traditional ganseys, *c.*1910.

Line-fishing for white fish was labour intensive and in winter the fishermen worked almost continuously for weeks at a time. At sea they only had an hour or two to sleep between baiting and shooting sixteen to eighteen miles of line carrying over 4,500 hooks, and hauling it in again to gut the fish and store it in ice. In summer, however, the boats often fished well over 100 miles from shore and the men would have time for a good sleep as the boat steamed home, to prepare them for the shore work of cleaning the boiler, trimming the coal bunkers, cleaning the boat's bottom and barking the gear (boiling it in a solution of cutch (oak or acacia bark) to preserve it).

BELOW DECKS

Probably owing to the fact that the skippers and crews owned the boats themselves, it was noted that the Scots took pride in the appearance of their boats: the funnels of steam drifters, for example, were regularly painted with bright colours. Below deck, however, cramped conditions and basic sanitary arrangements characterised the accommodation.

In the cabin, the men slept in narrow bunks built into the hull. *Boats' bedcla'es* were blankets sewn up together, perhaps with a cloth cover. It took a week for a new *c'aff seck* (straw mattress) to settle and mould to the shape of the body. On the first night at sea, what with the *c'aff seck*, blankets and feather pillow all stuffed into the tiny bunk there was barely room for the fisherman. Peter Buchan recalled - *Ye would ha'e t' fecht yer wye in then lie wi' yer nose scrapin' the deck, an' the caff aneth ye reeshlin' an' suekin' in the saick that wis fit t' burst.*

Kit used to carry provisions on board.

Below decks on the *Argonaut* KY257, 1957.

Several sets of clothing were carried in kists, including six sets of underwear and a new gansey for Saturday nights ashore. Washing facilities were minimal but it was important that the men have spare dry clothes. Meals were also taken in the cabin where a small luxury was the decorated china crockery many crews carried as their only concession to home comforts. However, little could be done to dispel the warm smell of engine oil and fish that clung to everything in the fuggy atmosphere.

There was little time for any activities other than work and sleep as there was always plenty to do. Although badly damaged nets were usually taken home for repair, running repairs had to be made on board to ensure that the boat had a full fleet of nets when they left for sea. The men could sleep in shifts while heading out to the fishing grounds or while the boat was lying at the nets. Then it was all hands to the ropes to haul in the catch.

FOOD

In the days of sail and steam, the fishermen's diet was simple and nourishing. Food had to be rich in calories (to provide the energy required for hard physical work) and easy to store and prepare in the cramped conditions of the galley.

Fish would be boiled or fried and eaten with oatcakes or potatoes. A big pan of *kail* (Scotch broth) would usually be bubbling away on the stove and sometimes a dumpling or duff (steamed pudding) would be cooked inside a tube within the kail pan to save space. *Crappit heids* was a traditional meal that involved packing fish livers and meal into a cod or haddock head or stomach and boiling them with fish flesh. Hard sea-biscuits were a plain but valuable alternative to bread.

A typical butcher's order for a trip to the lines (ten to twelve days) was:

2 x 5lbs roast beef	3 x 5 lbs boiling beef (for soup)
2 x 5 lbs stewing steak	3 x 5 lbs link sausages
2 x 5 lbs frying steak	50 slices of sausage meat
2 x 3lbs mince	10 lbs sliced bacon or ham

Eggs, bacon, sausage or porridge were served for breakfast, all washed down with copious quantities of strong, sweet tea.

For the long East Anglian herring season, every man took away a *Yermuth bun*, a large rich, fruit cake, and each Sunday one tin would be opened and the whole bun demolished at tea time.

By the early 20th century luxuries such as butter, jam and condensed milk were commonplace on board. On a trip to the West coast on board a Moray Firth drifter in the 1920s Peter F Anson enjoyed fried herring *that any first class chef would have been proud of,* and a *light and tasty plumduff.*

Kist used aboard the *White Cross* KY571.

The galley of the *Silver Chord* SY287, 1984.

POST-WAR FISHING

New technology changed the ways that fishermen worked on board. The increasing power and efficiency of fishing boats and their equipment, designed to enable fishermen to find and catch the maximum amount of fish, had benefits and also disadvantages for those at sea.

There have been significant advances in safety and comfort on board fishing boats in the last 50 years. Wheelhouses have developed from basic shelters to comfortable workstations. Better accommodation is provided in the men's cabins and galley, and much of the work that used to be done on deck is now completed under cover. Some of the largest vessels have carpeted cabins and fitness suites.

Increased mechanisation has also decreased the amount of manual work that the crews have to perform. Nets are no longer hauled by hand and the men no longer have to raise and lower massive sails. However, the introduction of mechanical equipment also brings danger simply because it is so powerful and the fishermen must be safety conscious at all times.

Having increasingly powerful equipment has brought new pressures. Because they are capable of it, boats are expected to travel further out to sea and stay there for longer. The fish are now generally processed on board and packed in ice, refrigerated or frozen; so removing the need to rush for home with the catch. This means longer trips away from home for the men. The modern drive for efficiency forces crews to snatch their shore leave in short bursts before heading off to sea once more to maximize their boat's takings during the season.

Government legislation and directives, particularly from the European Union, have influenced how long boats can spend at sea, what fish they can catch and how many. Fishing has always been an uncertain industry and this is as true now as it ever was. Increasing mechanisation has not been without its drawbacks. While conditions on board for fishermen have improved greatly, they still face daily dangers, uncertain earnings, and long periods away from home working in hostile conditions.

Andrianne INS8, Lochinver, 1992.

Gutting the catch on the *Argonaut IV* KY157, 1980s.

Safety At Sea

Fishing is one of the most dangerous occupations: even today it is common for twenty British fishermen to be killed each year. The sea itself is a dangerous environment. The weather can change very quickly bringing the obvious dangers of high winds and storms, but also less dramatic hazards such as fog and poor visibility. When the weather combines with sea conditions, such as currents, tides, and hidden obstacles like rocks, the result can be disaster.

Not all obstacles are natural ones. Many people use the sea and some areas are surprisingly crowded. The potential hazards a fisherman must avoid include cables, pipelines, oil and gas rigs, not to mention shipping lanes and military exercise zones. The dangers posed by other sea users are multiplied in times of war when fishermen may find their crews depleted, their fishing restricted and even themselves and their boats targeted.

On the deck of the *Argonaut IV* KY157, 1980s.

In addition, many of the dangers faced by fishermen at sea come, not from external forces, but from the day-to-day operating of powerful machinery in often unfavourable conditions. This is as true now as it was in the days of the sailing boats. In the days of sail, all of the work was done by hand and there was little or no protective clothing available. As fishing became more mechanised, the dangers on board grew. Machinery of the scale now in use on fishing boats is difficult enough to operate on land, in a dry, covered yard, let alone on a rolling vessel, more often as not, in the dark. In addition, fire and flood are constant dangers at sea.

Maritana **BCK408 on Ebb Carrs Rock, Eyemouth, 1927.**

The crew of the *Jacob George* YH176 being rescued by breeches buoy outside Eyemouth, *c.*1930.

Rotary foghorn.

FOLKLORE AND SUPERSTITIONS

The culture of mutual reliance in the face of great hardship and danger created a fiercely independent community with its own firm identity and customs. Fisherfolk were tight-knit and conservative, and their names, food and mode of life were different from the surrounding population. Even between different fishing villages there was often rivalry although occasionally marriages did take place between members of different communities brought together by travel to other ports.

Because of the dangerous nature of their work, fisherfolk were particularly superstitious. Thus there were words considered as very unlucky e.g. to mention the word minister was never done – he was called the man in the black coat. The words rabbit, salmon (red fish), rat (lang tail), pig (curly tail), and salt were amongst the most forbidden words. Should the men encounter a hare, a dog, or a person with red hair they were likely to refuse to put to sea and, if a rabbit, hare, dove, or pigeon were found on board they would most certainly not set out. The antidote to bad luck words was to touch *cauld iron*.

Other customs were associated with sailing or fishing itself. At Nairn it was unlucky to shoot nets on the port side, to taste food before the first fish was caught or not to take blood from the first fish. In some places fights were started so that blood could be shed before the fleet went to sea. Some boats were thought unlucky in themselves. One way of avoiding bad luck was never to row against the sun (anti-clockwise) when leaving harbour.

Rituals and charms were thought to influence the weather. It was believed that a wind could be whistled up or that it could be untied from special knots in a piece of rope: one knot would give a breeze, the second a gale and the third a storm. A change of weather was always expected on a Friday. In some areas, other days of the week had special significance, being either lucky or unlucky. Most communities did not fish on a Sunday for example, although it was considered a lucky day. Work begun on a Saturday was thought to take seven more Saturdays to complete while jobs started on Mondays would be finished quickly.

There were initiation customs before a lad could become a fisherman and, even now, customs and superstitions influence aspects of a fisherman's life. Echoes of the old ways are still found in the villages today.

Doll carried by Fisherrow Fishermen's Walk.

FISHERS OF MEN

Danger may draw men towards God but, on the other hand, at sea there are no ministers or churches. The unfair blows of fate and unpredictable earnings were as likely to drive men to the pub as to the kirk.

A change came in the fishing communities in 1859, a time of economic crisis, when the Revival Movement took root in Scotland. Its chief leader was Peterhead cooper James Turner who is said to have converted 8,000 people along the coasts in two years. From the 1880s, the Temperance Movement also had far-reaching effects. In some cases entire crews were converted and money that once had been spent on the bottle (up until the 1850s it was common for a curer to supply whisky to crews as part of their engagement) was now used to pay for improved gear and boats.

By the end of the 19th century most of the Protestant churches were involved in missions to fisherfolk. The Free Church, for example, established missions in Stornoway, Fraserburgh, Peterhead and Wick in 1898. In Lerwick a Baptist Mission was maintained until the 1930s. The fisherlasses, who represented a distinct group within the community, were especially targeted. Female church-workers known as *Biblewomen* distributed Christian literature and also acted as nurses, bandaging sores caused by gutting herring.

This was a common feature of the missions which acted as basic clinics and social clubs in addition to their spiritual function. As the fishergirls followed the fleets around the coast they, like the men, would often be living and working far away from home. The missions were a place where they could meet and socialise in relatively comfortable surroundings.

Sign board from Fraserburgh Mission Hall.

Mission Hall in Footdee, Aberdeen.

FISHERMEN AT WAR

Fishermen through the ages have faced a variety of dangers brought on by war. Indeed, they have often formed part of the first line of defence for the coasts of Britain.

There is evidence that both the attacks of the Spanish Armada and the earlier Dutch Wars had the effect of restricting the fishing, while Scottish fishermen and fishing vessels played a vital part in both World Wars I and II. During the First World War, fishermen and their vessels formed the backbone of the Royal Naval Reserve. Again in World War II around 10,000 of a total 17,000 Scottish fishermen served in the Royal and Merchant Navies and 670 fishing boats were commandeered by the Admiralty.

As active service vessels, fishing boats were a legitimate target for enemy submarines, gunships and aircraft. Those on patrol or mine-sweeping duties were fitted with weapons of their own to repel such attacks. However, other boats continued fishing to provide the population with a much-needed source of fresh food (fish was never rationed), and they too were vulnerable.

The dangers of war continue for fishermen long after hostilities have ceased. Unexploded mines planted by submarines are found even today and, if hauled up in nets, can sink a boat if not properly disposed of. The remnants of wartime defences also litter the seabed, including tank traps: large concrete blocks positioned around many of the beaches of east Scotland, many of which are invisible at high tide.

The *Trustful* on service as a hospital ship, Scapa Flow.

The *Girl Christian* armed for war service, 1940.

Fishermen on naval service during World War I.

SUPPORT ORGANISATIONS

Organisations were set up to save lives at sea, promote safety and to support fishermen and their families. These ranged from local Sea Box Societies (run and funded by subscription by the fishermen themselves to provide for widows and orphans of those lost at sea), to national or government agencies.

Some of the agencies currently operating in the UK are: the MAIB (Marine Accident Investigation Branch), which investigates marine accidents and publishes an annual Safety Digest, detailed accident reports, and statistics; the MCA (Maritime and Coastguard Agency), which was founded in the 18th century as part of the Board of Customs to prevent smuggling, and gradually took on a life-saving role using boats and shore-based apparatus to rescue people at sea; and the MSA (Marine Safety Agency), an executive agency of the Department of Transport which publishes safety information and regulations for fishermen and other sea users.

Their work is supplemented by charities such as the RNLI (Royal National Lifeboat Institution), a charity that was founded in 1824 as the National Institution for the Preservation of Life from Shipwreck. Its aim is to save lives at sea and it operates a fleet of lifeboats from over 230 stations around the coasts of Britain and Ireland; and the RNMDSF (Royal National Mission to Deep Sea Fishermen), a national Christian charity founded by Ebenezer J Mather in 1882. Its volunteers still provide material and spiritual support to fishermen, their families and communities at over 96 fishing harbours in the UK.

Crew of the lifeboat *The Royal Stuart*, 1900.

Launch of the lifeboat *James & Mary Walker*, Anstruther, 1904.

Anstruther's first lifeboat, *Admiral Fitzroy*, c.1870.

James Jack, coxwain of The Doctors by James Selbie.

Life Onshore

Although they rarely went to sea, fisherwomen were intimately connected with the work of the industry on shore. They often had more responsibility than their country counterparts, as they would run the home alone for long periods while the men were at sea and so had control of the family finances. In addition to their normal household duties they were responsible for collecting and preparing bait, mending nets and gear, preparing the fish for sale and hawking it on their backs around the district or, later, by train to neighbouring cities. In areas without harbours, they often helped to launch and beach the boats, and even to carry the men onboard to keep them dry.

Despite the severe poverty of previous years, the great boom in the herring industry was a time of prosperity for many fisher families and their standard of living would have compared favourably with agricultural workers. Fisherfolk were also unusual in having two-storey houses before many other workers. The need for a place to store and repair gear between fishing seasons meant that many fisherfolk preferred a house with a loft in which to undertake this work. Others would lease space in a commercial building to repair their gear.

Fishwife's creel.

In 1900 the balance between mass-production and hand-crafting was beginning to shift. Many of the items in the house, such as the range and the crockery, would have been manufactured while others including most of the wooden furniture and the cooking utensils would have been made in small local workshops. Other items such as some of the textiles or fishing gear would have been made by members of the family themselves.

Carrying the men to the boats, Portessie, *c.*1890.

THE HERRING BOOM

Loading herring for export at Peterhead, *c*.1910.

The herring fishing was at its most prosperous in the years before the First World War. It developed into a national industry: the various populations of herring around the coasts of Britain matured at different times creating a nationwide pattern of distinct seasons which the fleets followed. Along with them went the shore-workers who supplied the boats and processed the catch as it was landed.

By the mid 19th century, many fishing towns and villages were established around the coast of Scotland. This was especially true of the East coast where there were over 100 active fishing settlements between John O' Groats and Berwick Upon Tweed.

The proportion of shore-workers to fishermen varied from place to place but there were always many more jobs on land than at sea. By 1855 for example, Peterhead had over 1,000 coopers, Anstruther had 1,150 gutters and packers, and the herring fishing at Wick provided work for over 11,000 people during the season. In the same year at Burntisland, Fife, there were 23 fishermen supported by 189 coopers, gutters, packers, salesmen and net-makers while Fraserburgh had 295 fishermen to 1074 shore-workers.

These settlements provided the skilled labour needed to fully exploit the herring shoals around the coast. The herring season began in late May in the Hebrides and a fortnight later in Shetland. Through the summer, the fleets moved from Orkney and Shetland down the East coast until they reached Northumberland and Yorkshire by mid September. October to December saw them in Yarmouth and Lowestoft. Some boats also took part in a winter season: herring spawning in the Forth, Minch, Irish Sea and off Northern Island were fished from January to March.

By the early 1900s, a third of English herring landings were from Scottish boats and were cured by Scottish curers. In 1913 for example, 1,163 Scottish drifters fished off East Anglia and of the 12,000 Scottish women gutters, 5,000 travelled south (3,500 of these from the Hebrides).

Setting up the nets aboard steam drifters, Anstruther, 1938.

HERRING PACKING AT YARMOUTH

Curing yard at South Denes, Great Yarmouth *c.*1900.

THE HERRING LASSES

It was hard wark, but we widnae ha'e missed it

Packing herring barrels at Lowestoft, 1930s.

Herring gutters at Peterhead, *c.*1910.

Above: **Gutting herring at Stornoway, 1930s.**

Each year 6,000 Scots girls used to travel from port to port to gut and pack the herring.

Left: **St Monans fisherlasses at Yarmouth**

> O for Yarmouth bustle and hurry,
> Time for nothing but making money,
> But still it has its little joys,
> Hippodrome, theatre, Gem and Boys
>
> **Elizabeth Bain, Nairn herring lass**

> I had learned to gut when I was 10: curing had started in a big way. In 1844 during the summer, most Broadsea fishers went to the west coast and the Hebrides. We as lassies went to cook for the men. We lived in sodbuilt bothies on the shore... The work was hard for children, but we had a lot of fun. I enjoyed the long sail round the north of Scotland hugging the coast, I was with my father, and had faith in his skeelie seamanship.
>
> **Christian Watt, Broadsea herring lass**

> I suppose nowadays people would think the work was hard. But we were young and it was fun. We started at six o'clock in the morning, sometimes only half awake. We were supposed to work from six until nine at night but I've seen us working until one in the morning - I've seen us working until six in the morning, all through the night just to get the herring finished... It was a skilful job. You had to be quick and you had to get the gut out clean. If you took the head off that was no use, that fish was rejected.
>
> **Margaret Smith, Crovie herring lass**

Fife fisherlasses at Wick, 1930s with wedding flags flying.

We worked six days a week, never on a Sunday and we didn't usually gut on Monday - that day was used for what they called "filling up"... That was the day when we'd wash our oilskins; we'd put paraffin on them and scrub them to get rid of the fish grease. The boats did not go out until Monday afternoon and it was Tuesday morning before they came in with a fresh catch. Only the English boats went to sea on a Sunday at that time.

Margaret Smith, Crovie herring lass

Every finger had to be tied up. Idderwise da saat wid come atween wir fingers an rub. Da forefinger wis da worst. We alwyes hed ta hae a thick wan on wir forefinger because dat's whaar da knife ösed ta cut da bandage.

Christina Jackman, Shetland herring lass

We never worked on Saturday nichts because dat wis da nicht we gied ta da dance... we wid geng oot an we wid be picking da scales aff wir arms as we gied alang, an wi da heat a da ballroom da chaps smelt da herring in wir hair. It didna matter how much time we washed wir hair, it alwyes smelt...

Christina Jackman, Shetland herring lass

Because herring was an oily fish, it had to be cured as quickly as possible to prevent it rotting. There were different methods of curing: white herring was packed in barrels with salt; red herring was smoked over oak fires for up to a month before packing. White herring was the more usual Scottish product, but the quality varied before the introduction of standards in the 19th century.

The Scottish Fisheries Act of 1815 set down certain standards for cured herring. The fish had to be gutted with a sharp knife (known as a *futtle*) and packed in salt within 24 hours of being caught. Only herring cured to this standard were awarded the *Crown Brand* by the Fishery Officer.

The women who carried out this work came from every fishing town from Stornoway to Eyemouth. They were recruited by representatives of the curers who paid them *arles*. This money acted as a contract for the season and the going rate in the period before 1914 was £1. The curer also paid them a weekly wage to cover their lodgings and food, and provided oilskins and boots. Each girl tied on her own finger cloths or *cloots* to protect her hands from the salt water and slips of the knife.

The women worked out of doors at the *farlans* (large wooden troughs) in crews of three: two gutters and one packer. The gutters were responsible for gutting the fish and grading them according to size. An experienced gutter was expected to process sixty fish a minute and a packer aimed to fill three barrels an hour. Working until midnight was not unknown when the fishing was good as each day's catch had to be cleared before the next catch came in. The women were paid according to the amount of fish they processed so they worked as hard as they could to keep their earnings up. They considered £17 or £20 a good income for a season.

The fish were examined before the cooper closed the barrels. After ten days each barrel was re-examined and filled up as necessary before final sealing. This was the *Scotch Cure*. Strict quality control, led by the Fishery Officer, was encouraged by the curers who could get excellent prices for high quality herring. This ensured the dominance of the Scotch Cure in the Eastern European market prior to the First World War.

Gutting Herring **by John McGhie RA.**

A PLACE TO STAY

In the resorts of Yarmouth and Lowestoft the herring lasses lived in lodgings in town. However, in Shetland they lived in purpose-built huts at the curing stations.

Lodgings could vary from being comfortable to very primitive. While landladies could see the benefit of earning income from lodgers in the off-season, the price was the mess caused by the herring. Yarmouth landladies would lift carpets and cover walls in brown paper to try to counteract the lingering smell of fish. All would be returned to normal for the summer tourists once the lasses had gone. If a lass found good lodgings she would try to return to the same place each season.

Living in huts gave the women more freedom although conditions were basic. Many huts were used as barrel stores in the off-season so the women's first job when they reached the yards was to clean them out, paper the walls and put up some decorations. A corner was curtained off as a *glory hole*. The hut would have bunk-beds and a fireplace, for which the curer provided coal. Each lass brought her personal belongings with her in a kist. These would be clothes and also some home comforts to make the huts more comfortable.

The women took it in turns to light the fire, fetch water and do the cooking for the hut. At weekends they would bake buns and so on to entertain the fishermen home from the sea. The crews would often be men from the women's home towns who had also travelled with the fleets. The social aspect of life in the huts was one of its main attractions and many girls met their future husbands while working at the curing yards.

Contents of the Kist:

Working and Sunday clothes
Sheets
Towels
Knitting wool, needles and belt (*wiska*)
Cups and saucers
Tablecloth
Bandages
Gutting knife
Oilskin coat

Also taken:

Chaff-filled mattress (*caff-seck*)
Pillows
Blankets
Working boots

Huts formerly used by herring gutters, Shetland, 1984.

KNITTING

Fisherwomen were famous for their knitting. For a woman to sit *haund-idle* was a crime and they would knit while walking, visiting friends, when *crackin' wi the neebors* at the door or even during a break in the herring yards. When the men left for the fishing season they took sea-kists packed with hand-knitted garments – five or six of each:

Pittenweem lasses at Yarmouth, *c*.1900.

GANSEYS

Guernseys or ganseys were knitted in un-oiled, soft, round, dark-blue 6 or 5 ply wool on size 14 needles to make a firm, close fabric that was almost wind and waterproof. Some traditions state that a drowned man could be identified by the pattern on his gansey. The patterns had names such as *herring bone*, *anchor* and *flag* and could be varied or combined according to taste. Women moving from port to port copied each other's designs and could even copy a pattern seen being worn by a stranger in the street.

Fisherman's gansey.

DRAWERS

Drawers or long-johns were knitted in wheeling wool (a thick but slightly open twist) in a pinkish colour called Shetland Grey. Size 12 needles were used to give a softer garment and cotton fabric used to make a wide waistband and lining in the crotch-gusset.

SEABOOT STOCKINGS

These went over the trouser legs and were also made of wheeling wool in dark greys and heather mixtures, like the knee-high work socks.

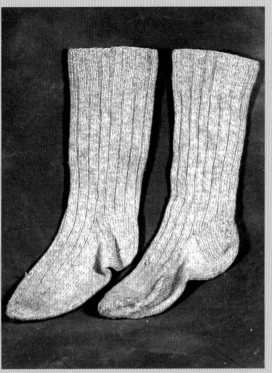

MITTENS, SCARVES AND *GUID* SOCKS FOR SUNDAY

Sunday socks were made from fingering wool, smooth and closely spun in 5 or even 4 ply for special occasions. Girls of ten or twelve could tackle mittens or socks and had often learned to knit Shetland shawls by the time they left school at thirteen, for the women had to knit for themselves and the children, as well as for the men.

As far as possible, knitting was done in the round on four double-ended steel needles so that stitching up was not necessary. A knitting belt or *wiska* was often used as an extra hand to hold the needles.

So expert were the knitters that they replaced worn stocking toes or heels, knees or seats of drawers almost invisibly. They had no printed instructions: patterns and sizes, tricks and techniques were all learned by example.

Fisherlasses knitting while at Lowestoft.

THE COOPER

The coopers made the thousands of barrels required each year to cure and keep the herring. In the curing yards they were also responsible for quality control. The cooper saw that the barrels were drained of brine after the initial packing of herring had settled. He then closed the barrels after adding more fish and brine.

The barrels themselves were made from Scandinavian spruce and their size was fixed at $26\,^{2/3}$ Imperial gallons. The coopers would serve a four year apprenticeship before becoming qualified. Barrels had to be made to a high standard so that they were completely air and watertight: a well-packed and sealed barrel of herring would keep for a year or more. The wooden staves were shaped using special tools with curved blades. They were held in position around a smouldering fire of shavings which warmed the wood and made it easier to bend. The metal hoops were then hammered into place and the ends finished off before the lids were cut and fitted.

Barrel stencil for Cormack of Wick.

Coopers *c.*1889.

In his role as inspector, the cooper checked the gutters' selection of the different kinds of herring so that the barrels contained only one type. There were seven categories of fish from *matties* (immature herring) to *large fulls* (fully grown fish that had not yet spawned) and this information was branded onto the barrel lid along with the curer's stamp.

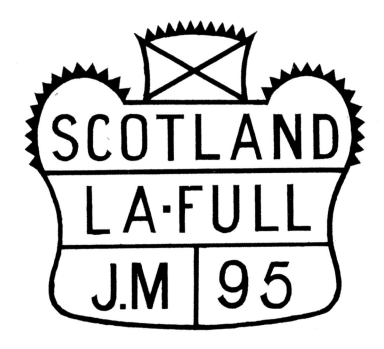

FISHERY BOARD FOR SCOTLAND.

I. IMPRESSIONS OF OFFICIAL CROWN BRANDS.

"LARGE FULL."

For Herrings with roe or

milt not less than

$11\frac{1}{4}$ inches in extreme

length.

The cooper would accompany the Fishery Officer on quality inspection rounds, hoping for the coveted *Crown Brand*. Some curers gained such a reputation that their stamp was recognised as almost equal to the Crown Brand. Coopers also escorted buyers with huge orders for Russia and Germany who would demand that a random selection of barrels be opened. They would test the herring by breaking them and tasting a bite of the half-cured fish.

A skilled cooper might make seventy barrels a week. They tended to make barrels between the seasons, although many more might be required if the landings were good. Some coopers went on to become curers, employing coopers and herring lasses of their own.

CURERS, SALESMEN AND AUCTIONEERS

In the 19th century, curers and merchants were the central figures in the chain between fishermen and customers. Prior to the 1880s, fishermen were engaged for the season by a curer, usually a former cooper, who would pay for equipment, boat maintenance and provisions in advance. In return, the fishermen would sell their fish to him for a pre-arranged price for catches up to an agreed level (usually 200 crans per season).

However, increased efficiency brought massive numbers of herring to the markets. This caused a slump in prices and curers, bound by the agreements, lost money. Therefore, an open market system of auctioning was introduced on the East Anglian model. This resulted in more risk to fishermen in poor years but more share of the bounty when prices were high.

Peterhead was the first Scottish port to abandon the engagement system in favour of public auctions held in the newly built fish market in the late 1880s. The new fish salesmen stepped in to replace the curers as providers of loans to fishermen for gear and so on. Their income depended on commissions on sales from the boats they represented so they had a personal interest in maximising catches. Each harbour would have its local firms, such as W Aitken, Fish Merchant, of Anstruther alongside offices of national companies such as Cormack's of Wick.

A fish sale at St. Monans, 1930s.

When the fish were landed, a sample would be taken to the auctioneer who would display it on his pulpit. He would ring his bell to call the buyers to the ring where they would bid, depending on the quality and size of the catch. The freshest fish fetched the highest prices so boats would race back to port. Poor catches forced prices up while demand was strong. From the auction the fish would go to the curing yards to be gutted and packed.

Salesmen who provided loans for boats usually acted as agents for them, selling the catch and keeping the accounts as well as paying bills for supplies. However, they had the old problem of being the first to feel the effects of a poor season in unpaid bills and there are records of smaller firms being unable to survive a poor winter.

GAUN AWA' SOOTH

The East Anglian fishing was the crown of the year for the herring drifters, and folk said of the fishermen: *Oh aye! They a' get the herrin' fivver come October.* By the turn of the 20th century, the annual trip south was an established part of the herring season and Scottish steam drifters were an accustomed sight in the ports of Yarmouth and Lowestoft.

The boats would not all leave together but in groups depending on the tide. Children, allowed out of school for an hour, joined the small crowd around their father's boat. The mate *gi'ed oot the bakes*, a small handful of ships' biscuits, to those gathered on the pier, then everyone hurried to the harbour mouth to cheer and throw pennies on the decks as the boats, with sirens whooping, sailed out and away.

The return of the fleet in late November or early December was an even more exciting time because it was from Yarmouth that the fisherfolk got their main presents of the year. Until the late 1930s, Scots paid little attention to Christmas. Instead, from Yarmouth came the big dolls and tricycles, Meccano sets and chatterboxes, chocolates and perfumes, even fox-furs and gold bracelets. Some years brought more unusual gifts if the boats landed herring at Ijmuiden on the Dutch coast and the fishermen returned with boxes of fat cigars, glass tea-trays and Delftware patterned with windmills.

Word would come by telegram that the boats had left and the children would watch from garret windows and sea walls until their own boat came in. The harbour would be a bustle for days with carts carrying gear and kists home and nets drying on the gallowses, while the wash-boilers were on for days on end.

The women took out their net needles and mending shears to prepare the gear for the next season: *or they'll nivver be dune for the new 'ear for next 'ear'll hae enough a-dae wi' itsel.*

A typical gift brought home at the end of the season.

Sending off the fleet: *Violet* KY251 leaving Anstruther, 1930s.

Fishing Communities In The 21st Century

Traditional smoking shed, Arbroath, 2003.

In recent years the fishing industry has seen a period of rapid change that has resulted in a huge decline in the number of fishing boats and fishermen operating from Scotland (around 200 vessels were lost from the fleet between 2002 and 2008, largely as a result of government-sponsored decommissioning). Concerns about over-fishing and the impact of EU regulations have resulted in a shift away from traditional fishing methods to smaller scale, inshore fishing and fish farming.

The prawn fleet at Pittenweem, 2001.

Scottish fishermen still operate but the offshore fleets are concentrated in the larger ports such as Peterhead and Fraserburgh. Activity in smaller harbours is confined to prawn trawling or creeling. Women still play a part, often working in fish processing factories or in fish shops or vans selling the catch. However, the fishing industry, in parallel with the wider economy, is increasingly reliant on migrant workers who take jobs in the factories or as crew. They are considered harder working and more reliable than many locals who no longer see fishing, with all its hardships and uncertainties, as a good career.

This has had an impact on the nature of fishing communities. Descendants of fisher families often now move away for work or find jobs in the tourist industry that has replaced fishing as the main employer in many harbours. However, some fisher families still follow their forebears into the industry and Scottish yards still build new boats every year to maintain the fleet. Community events also continue to bring people together to recall the past and celebrate the distinctive character of Scotland's coastal towns and villages.

The Scottish Fisheries Museum

THE SITE AND BUILDINGS

The museum is centred on a courtyard which constitutes part of the original land which was gifted by the then Laird of Anstruther, William de Candela, to the Abbot of Balmerino (in North Fife) in 1318. The Abbot subsequently leased the area to the local townsfolk to enable them to sell or cure their fish, to dry and repair their gear and to bark their lines and nets in order to prevent rotting by exposure to salt water. In return, the Abbey was given a barrel of one hundred salt herring from each of the townsfolk's catches.

ST. AYLES CHAPEL

In the 16th century, a small chapel was built on the northern side of the courtyard. We have no definite explanation of the origin of the name although it may be a corruption of St. Adrian. After the Reformation, the building fell into disrepair and was eventually dismantled to make way for the construction of a storehouse.

Memorial to Scottish fishermen lost at sea.

THE ABBOT'S LODGING

This building on the east side of the Courtyard was built by a Thomas Wood after the land was leased to him by the Abbey. In return the Abbot used it as a residence while staying overnight on his pilgrimages to the May Isle (an important religious shrine dedicated to St. Adrian and on the pilgrim route to St. Andrews).

THE MERCHANT'S HOUSE

On the west side, can be seen an old merchant's house, dating from the 18th century. This eventually became a ship chandler's business.

THE MUSEUM AND COLLECTIONS

The Museum houses a collection that was one of the first ten in Scotland, outside the National Museums, to be designated as a 'Recognised Collection of National Significance'. It provides a full and fascinating history of the industry and its communities around the Scottish coast. Many of the objects can be viewed seven days a week throughout the year. The reserve collection, library/research centre and archives are available by appointment.

The Museum's boat collection of 19 full-sized vessels is the centrepiece and contains three boats on the register, two in the core collection, of the Historic Ships Committee – the Fifie *Reaper*, the Zulu *Research* and the ring-netter *Lively Hope*. The *Reaper* and *White Wing* regularly attend maritime events around Scotland and *Reaper* has been as far south as Portsmouth. These are complemented by the model boat collection that is the most comprehensive of its kind in Scotland.

Above: **Model of the seine-netter *Argonaut IV* built in 1976.**

Model boats displayed in the Wheelhouse Gallery.

There are over 12,000 items of fishing vessel equipment and gear relating to fishing and whaling. This is complemented by a similarly comprehensive collection of the tools of trades associated with the industry, like coopering. Natural history is represented mainly by the Buckland collection of fish casts and a small but important collection of items relating to whaling and sealing.

Quarter-cran herring measure.

Detail of a drifter's messenger rope.

Detail of a line basket.

Gimbal compass.

The Museum collects items of social and domestic life from fishing communities around Scotland, but particularly from the East Neuk. The costume collection contains over 1,000 items worn by fishermen and women and these are frequently used for research purposes. These include oilskin aprons, as worn by the herring gutters, gala outfits and accessories through to contemporary workwear.

Visitors sampling life as a fisherlass.

Fine art is well represented by examples in different media and ranges from highly regarded artists like John McGhie to the so-called amatuer 'pier-head painters'. The Thomas Thomson collection contains a particularly fine array of watercolours. The substantial photographic collection of over 13,000 negatives and 5,000 slides are constantly being added to. They are invaluable for research, family history enquiries and illustrative material for publications. The archives contain oral history recordings, films, documents, business records, charts and plans from boat-builders, such as J.N. Miller and Sons of St. Monans.

The collection is rich and varied in range and depth and represents the single most important source for the study of the history of the fishing industry in Scotland.

Landing Herring at Anstruther **by Franc P Martin, 1930.**

Fishwife motif popularised by Queen Victoria.

Advertisement, *c.*1870.